Mozart
Traces of Transcendence

D1352886

MOZART

Traces of Transcendence

Hans Küng

SCM PRESS LTD
London

Translated by John Bowden from
Mozart. Spuren der Transzendenz,
published 1991 by Piper Verlag, Munich

© R. Piper GmbH & Co. KG, Munich 1991

Translation © John Bowden 1992

ISBN 0 334 02179 0

First British edition published 1992 by
SCM Press Ltd,
26–30 Tottenham Road, London, N1 4BZ

Phototypeset at The Spartan Press Ltd, Lymington, Hants
and printed in Great Britain by
Mackays of Chatham, Kent

Contents

Foreword
by Sir Yehudi Menuhin

'Le cœur a ses raisons que la raison ne connaît point.' Hans Küng, in his admirable dissertation on Mozart's profound awareness of faith as of belief, lays bare the eternal contradiction of life – that between human certainties and eternal truth.

Human certainties are eminently fallible and eternal truth unknowable, yet undeterred we seek assurance, authority, security and infallibility. Man is, by definition, a religious animal, whether he believes in Christ or anti-Christ, whether he believes in God or man as supreme, whether espousing communism or the free market, whether intent on massacring or saving – whilst as 'les extrêmes se touchent' he is also a doubter, harbouring the very contradictions he seeks to resolve or to reconcile: 'Lord, I believe, help Thou mine unbelief.' The Son of God on the cross in his agony asks the Father – his, our Father – 'My God, my God, why hast Thou forsaken me?' 'Eli, Eli, lama sabachthani?'

Certainties bring critical assessments in their wake as well as condemnation and hypocrisy.

Hans Küng has done well to restore the heart of faith and belief to their essential purity – including the symbolic order together with the symbolic words of the Mass, eternally independent of the trenchant trappings of any particular usage, dogma, catechism or theology.

Mozart's together with his father's adoption of the Masonic Order was both a recognition of high principles in a temporal order as it was a revolt against their own personal experience of the abuse by church dignitaries of their temporal power and their betrayal of Christian values.

This act by Mozart can surely be interpreted as an assertion, a confirmation of his true and pure faith, while in no way denying his abiding sensuality. May the joy, reverence and compassion ever present in Mozart's divine music be reflected in our daily lives, always be so perceived by our hearts, our bodies and our minds, and ever dwell in our spirits.

Yehudi Menuhin
June 1992

Preface

Much has been written about Wolfgang Amadeus Mozart, but relatively little about the religious dimension of his person and his music. In this slim volume I shall attempt to make rather deeper theological soundings into Mozart's musical work, in two directions.

Part One begins with the question of the Catholic background of Wolfgang Amadeus Mozart, something which surprisingly enough has hardly been discussed by Mozart scholars. It is completely taken for granted that Johann Sebastian Bach has Protestant roots and was a pious man, and that his work therefore has a religious quality. Yet the question of Mozart's religious background is regarded as a very different matter. However, as we know, the world-view to which people are brought up and the atmosphere that they breathe in church or religion are quite decisive for an understanding of them. And on that basis we can ask the deeper theological question whether and to what degree Mozart's music itself (not just his church music, but his instrumental music in particular) displays 'traces of transcendence' – though these may be perceptible only to those who want to hear them. I shall argue that in Mozart's music something can sometimes appear which goes beyond the human dimension and gives intimations of the mystery of a 'bliss' which transcends even all music. Without 'divinizing' the human, all-too-human, person of Wolfgang Amadeus Mozart and commandeering his music for theology, I shall attempt here to describe experiences with music which, even if they do not 'prove' anything, are nevertheless open in the direction of transcendence.

Part Two similarly makes an unusual attempt, namely to consider Mozart's Coronation Mass in the light of its contemporary cultural and political horizon and at the same time to set it against the critical confrontation with religion which was already beginning at that time. This approach highlights some striking tensions: the texts of the mass on the one hand and at the same time, on the other, their negation by the modern criticism of religion which puts any religion in question. Is not Mozart's church music, like religion generally, 'opium of the people'? Here not only does Mozart's critical attitude to church authority come out clearly, but also the ambivalence of any criticism of religion, and finally the possibility of a new creative understanding of the texts as interpreted by Mozart's music.

Part One was written in response to an invitation by August Everding, the Director of the Prinzregenten Theatre in Munich, to give a celebratory lecture at the beginning of 1991, the Mozart jubilee year. I repeated this lecture on various occasions: at a meeting of the Catholic Academy in Freiburg im Breisgau, during the International Music Festival in Lucerne, at the opening of the Mozart Symposium in Salzburg sponsored by Austrian Radio, and finally at a Mozart concert given by the Tübingen Collegium Musicum at the University of Tübingen.

Part Two was written in response to an invitation by Dr Erwin Koller of Swiss Television and Kapellmeister Armin Brunner of Radio Bremen to give a theological meditation on Mozart's Coronation Mass which was presented during a concert performance of this mass on television. The text printed here is the epic longer version, which was the basis for the rather more rhetorical shorter version given during the television performance.

Behind the whole book lies a lifetime of listening to Mozart's music. Even so, it could not have been written without all the valuable criticism and stimulation which I have received from my musicological colleagues: I am particularly grateful to the composer Professor Karl Michael Komma; to Professors Arnold Feil and Manfred Hermann Schmid, both at the University of Tübingen; and to Professor Helmut Hucke of the University of Frankfurt.

Tübingen, July 1991   Hans Küng

Traces of Transcendence?

Experiences with Mozart's Music

The organizer of this bicentenary celebration of the death of Wolfgang Amadeus Mozart took no small risk when instead of a musician or a musicologist he invited simply a committed hearer – I am no more than that, nor do I seek to be – to give the commemorative lecture. It may be an excuse for the organizer and a relief to the speaker that Mozart himself – although according to Haydn's famous saying he was 'the greatest composer' with the 'most profound knowledge of composition'[1] – sometimes enjoyed improvising at length before ordinary people and in the end did not write his music for music scholars, but for committed hearers of every kind.

Two figures stand out among these committed hearers who have been intensively preoccupied with Mozart all their lives, each of them with their own special experiences with his music. Although neither of them was a music scholar, they both gave much-noted commemorative addresses during the celebrations marking the bicentenary of Mozart's birth in 1956, which were then published in more or less extended versions under the simple titles 'Mozart' or 'Wolfgang Amadeus Mozart'. With the profundity of their reflections and the brilliance of their presentation, both authors have set very high standards for addresses commemorating Mozart.

The first was Karl Barth, the only great theologian of the twentieth century to plumb Mozart's work theologically, in its tremendous range and quantity.[2]

The second was Wolfgang Hildesheimer, the most musically sensitive German author of our time. He attempted to uncover the original portrait of Mozart, the man and the artist, from under the many subsequent over-paintings of a history which has now continued uninterrupted for two hundred years.[3]

I see myself somewhere between these two admirers of Wolfgang Amadeus Mozart. I have a personal acquaintance with both Karl Barth the church dogmatic theologian and Wolfgang Hildesheimer, the sceptical man of letters, and respect them deeply. Yet in speaking about Mozart, I think that there is one advantage that I have over this theologian of Protestant origin and this agnostic of Jewish origin. As you know, I too am a Catholic. Could not some reflection on Mozart's whole Catholic background, which so far has hardly been discussed as a specific theme, make a very small contribution towards understanding him? I am convinced that this background may be at least of some importance, so that is where I begin my 'Divertimento teologico'.

Theme 1:
Catholic?

Both my revered conversation partners were virtually forced to take note of Mozart's Catholicism.

The Protestant theologian was almost apologetic for dealing in his *Church Dogmatics* with a musician who was not 'a particularly active Christian, and was a Roman Catholic',[4] a musician, moreover, who obviously thought that Protestants had their religion too much 'in their heads'.[5]

Wolfgang Hildesheimer is very reluctant to concede Mozart's Catholic heritage: 'On the surface (!) and above all seen in retrospect (!), Mozart was a "Catholic phenomenon" (!), raised in an area in which (atmospherically, geographically and philosophically) faith ruled life . . .'[6] To which Hildesheimer also adds: 'Or are we in error about this, too? Do we overestimate the power of customs peculiar to certain historical periods? Probably.'[7]

So was Wolfgang Amadeus Mozart at best a 'Catholic' in quotation marks, on the surface, conditioned by his time, unavoidably? The question of Mozart's church background, which is barely discussed in the Mozart literature,[8] is not just relevant to Mozart's church music. Was Mozart really Catholic? At least his Salzburg Archbishop Colloredo may have had considerable doubts about this, regardless of the fact that the infant prodigy had been awarded a papal order at a very early age. For did this rebellious and often witty musician really hold the Catholic truth in theory and practice 'without reduction' and 'integrally', as the great lords used to put it in those days? Certainly Mozart – like Franz Schubert after him – never stinted himself in the music in the *Credo* of the mass which referred to the church: the *unam sanctam catholicam et apostolicam ecclesiam*. But any official approval of his Catholic faith by the church which the young Konzertmeister of the Salzburg Hofkapelle might have needed on his appointment in 1769 would have been withdrawn again by his archbishop at the latest in 1777, when the twenty-one-year-old Wolfgang, who had developed an increasing antipathy to the episcopal city, on being refused absence of leave asked to be released from his post. For as is well known, the archbishop reacted by dismissing Wolfgang's father Leopold as well! At best the rebellious composer, who wanted no longer to be dependent on the bishop but to have both civic and artistic independence, could have counted himself among the critical Catholics when he had definitely broken with his archbishop in Vienna in 1781. While Count Arco, the archbishop's Master of the Kitchen, did not excommunicate Wolfgang, he did literally kick him out. From now on Mozart, as he himself put it, 'hated the archbishop to madness'.[9] Truly, the story of Mozart and the Bishop of Salzburg is a notoriously painful one – for the latter, it should be noted – but we need not relate it in detail here.[10]

In short, neither episcopal-clerical Salzburg nor imperial-feudal Vienna in the least supported Mozart to the degree that he deserved, and even art-loving Munich, where he had given a concert at the early age of six, did not want to keep him even after the performance of *Idomeneo* in 1781. And once Mozart, who by upbringing and nature was hardly political, had written enthralling music in Vienna for Beaumarchais' and da Ponte's *Figaro*, with its subversive criticism of society, presenting the great lord as bad and all the rest as good, that was that. The aristocracy increasingly followed the clergy, with whom they had close links, in rejecting the non-conformist composer. There were no more church commissions (no occasion for completing the great C Minor Mass, a great work in every respect), and very few commissions from the court and the nobility – apart from dance music and divertimenti. The funeral music for the Masonic lodge which Mozart had joined in 1784 despite the papal condemnation of the Masons by Clement XII in 1738 (Haydn was also a member) was of course no substitute.[11]

Be this as it may, it is enough here to note that all those interpreters are right who stress that in no way, given the prevailing circumstances, was Mozart a 'committed churchgoer', as present-day terminology has it, or even a conservative Catholic. With his affirmation of the Masonic ideal of human love and the Enlightenment, of freedom, equality and brotherhood, he had virtually no interest in the church as a hierarchical institution which often encouraged superstition and tolerated a decadent monasticism. However, may we conclude from this that this selfsame Mozart was not a believer?

Theme 2:
Religious?

Indeed, may we go so far as Wolfgang Hildesheimer? He claims:

that Mozart, at any rate 'in his church music, with perhaps some exceptions, phrases in the text which may have moved him deeply, beyond the mere liturgical context . . . did not have his mind on the job';

that there can be no question of his works being the 'creative expression of a confession of faith';[12]

that even in the case of a work like *Ave verum corpus* in D major (KV 618, 17 June 1791) it would be 'at the very least risky to regard this work as a sign of religious fervour';

that this work in particular testifies only to 'unqualified objectivity, the control of someone not involved';[13]

indeed, that Mozart's life 'is made up of roles to which he unconsciously adapts himself, giving his best to whatever subject is posed for him', so that 'in this case, too, role and incarnation and ego have become one'; 'a mysterious double life, and yet only apparently so'.[14]

My question here would be whether all too much of the religious scepticism of modern interpreters has not been transferred to the person being interpreted. Of course, critics nowadays rightly reject any sentimental reading of Mozart's works; with no historical figure should the boundaries between wish and reality, information and speculation be blurred. However, a neglect of the deepest levels of great music and allergies to anything religious should be equally intolerable to an objective reconstruction.

Granted, Mozart, who does not seem to have paid serious attention to landscape or history, art, literature or politics, may not in fact have been very impressed by Austrian and South German baroque architecture and festive, colourful liturgical ceremonies, at least if his letters are anything to go by. But which of us would like to be judged solely from our letters?

Granted, like so many organists, the Salzburg court organist went to church primarily for the sake of the music; he lived his life in the sphere of music and almost only in music. But does all this mean that Mozart, who according to his own testimony composed in his head, who went around all day with his mind on music, and was fond of speculating, studying and considering before rapidly writing it all down, was fundamentally irreligious and that even his church music was at best 'superficially' Catholic?

Granted, Mozart had little truck with church piety and hated popish practices. But on the other hand we have his own comment that he did not 'fully trust'[15] people without religion, and did not want to go on journeys or establish long-term friendships with them.[16]

Granted, the few Jews whom Mozart knew, Baron Wetzlar and his librettist da Ponte, were converted and hardly recognizable any longer to him as Jews. But may we say over and above that that the Catholic Mozart 'probably never perceived Protestants as such; at least he never comments on them'?[17] That at least is not the case. For if one's research is thorough one should not overlook, or perhaps want to overlook, the fact that in 1789, the year of the Revolution, Mozart had lively conversations with, among others, no less a figure than the then cantor of the Thomas-Kirche, Johann Friedrich Doles. All we have of this conversation is Mozart's remarkable statement that these 'enlightened Protestants' could probably never really understand what the '*Agnus Dei qui tollis peccata mundi, dona nobis pacem*, and the like' ('Lamb of God, who takes away the sins of the world, give us peace') meant to him.[18]

Unlike Hildesheimer, Karl Barth at least took note of this statement, but with furrowed brow and without going to the heart of Mozart's criticism.[19] Is this manifest repression perhaps the reason why Wolfgang Amadeus Mozart appeared to Barth in a dream? That is no legend. As he himself bears witness, the great dogmatic theologian once dreamed in all earnestness that he had had to examine Mozart in theology at the University of Basel, well aware that in no circumstances would Mozart be allowed to fail. (It should be mentioned in passing that Mozart would never have settled in Protestant Basel. Mozart always wanted to live 'no matter where, provided it be in a Catholic country'.[20]) To Barth's question what 'dogma' and 'dogmatics' were, 'despite my most friendly prompting and my hints about your masses', Mozart had given 'no answer at all'.[21] Why? Because the author of the monumental thirteen-volume *Church Dogmatics* had asked him about the dogmas of the church instead of about good Catholic religious experience – of which Mozart had spoken in connection with the *Agnus Dei* (and we shall hear more of this later).

By now Karl Barth may have had the opportunity to put the question directly to Mozart in heaven. At any rate, in connection with the story of his dream he confessed that if he, Barth, ever got to heaven (and post-conciliar Catholics assume this as a matter of course), there he would 'first of all seek out Mozart and only then inquire after Augustine, St

Thomas, Luther, Calvin, and Schleiermacher'.[22] Why? Because, Barth thinks, in Mozart more than any one else one can perceive an 'art of playing' which presupposes a 'childlike awareness of the essence or centre – as also the beginning and the end – of all things'.[23]

'An awareness of the centre – as also the beginning and the end – of all things.' It is easy to imagine why such a highly theological assertion by my fatherly theological friend on the right wing must seem at best 'touching' to my esteemed conversation partner on the left (as he recently told me). For Hildesheimer, Barth's interpretation is pious wishful thinking. Moreover, these two Mozart admirers, so unlike each other, have hardly ever acknowledged each other's existence where Mozart is concerned. Only at one point does Hildesheimer quote Barth, namely the famous comment that Barth is not absolutely certain 'that when the angels go about their task of praising God, they play only Bach', but that he is sure 'that when they are together *en famille*, they play Mozart and that then too the good God listens with special pleasure'.[24] On such a picture of God Hildesheimer remarks, sarcastically raising the question of theodicy, that in Barth's picture, 'I see God like Rembrandt's Saul enjoying the music of David's harp, lost in the thought that one ought perhaps to have done something for this divine musician during his earthly life.'[25]

However, I do not want yet to intervene in this dispute, but first of all to open up the substantive question on which all Mozart interpretation focusses and which is so infinitely difficult to answer. How is the phenomenon of Mozart to be described? What is so special about Mozart? Are not perhaps religious categories also needed if we are to grasp the specific character of this figure who is as fascinating as he is mysterious?

Theme 3:
Divine?

Indeed, great representative Mozart scholars have not hesitated to draw on religious vocabulary to interpret this unique phenomenon. For Alfred Einstein, Mozart was 'only a visitor upon this earth'.[26] A performing artist like Josef Krips sees Mozart not only reaching heaven with his works but even coming from there. Many interpreters speak of Mozart as being 'more than earthly', 'not of this world', 'divine'. Even Hans Werner Henze once spoke of the 'God come down from heaven',[27] and the Catholic theologian Hans Urs von Balthasar enthuses over Mozart's ascension into heaven: Mozart ascends 'above as a transfigured self with body and soul to the sounds of the *Magic Flute*', so that willy-nilly he seems to parallel the Risen Christ.[28]

In view of such metaphysical exaggeration there is perhaps a need for the sobriety of critical theology if we are to achieve the right perspective. Karl Barth at any rate always tried to avoid the sloppy word 'divine' (even Hildesheimer speaks of Mozart the 'divine performer'). This avoidance arises out of a justified anxiety about any kind of divinization of a human being which particularly in art all too easily degenerates from the divinization of the master to the divinization of the performer and especially the divinization of the diva. Karl Barth, who understood God as *totaliter aliter*, the 'wholly other', would not allow the attribute 'divine' even for his Wolfgang Amadeus Mozart.[29] And it is a credit to Mozart himself that he modestly entered his last and towering symphony, later called the 'Jupiter' symphony with a clear reference to its almost divine greatness, in his personal list of works as 'a symphony' (10 August 1788).

But if not divine, then what? One can hear on all sides that he was a 'wonder', a prodigy. That is said even by Goethe, who at the age of fourteen had heard the seven-year-old Mozart play in Frankfurt. I would prefer to refer directly to Wolfgang's father Leopold Mozart, of whom such a saying has been handed down with an additional phrase: Wolfgang was a wonder 'which God (!) had caused to be born in Salzburg'.[30] But does that take us a step further in explaining the phenomenon of Mozart? Hardly: for neither Mozart's father, the extremely cautious music teacher, nor his most competent contemporary admirer, Joseph Haydn, who was quite without envy, sought to describe this 'wonder' precisely. Indeed, it has proved difficult even for the greatest representatives of musicology – above all Hermann Abert and Alfred Einstein – to describe just what it is that makes Mozart Mozart.

Granted, from the music of Mozart, who even as a child indefatigably kept practising, learning and studying everywhere, one could and can establish the roots of his style and all kinds of influences on him: first from Leopold Mozart, then from Schubert, Wagenseil, Gluck, Sammartini, Piccini, Paisiello, and above all from Bach's youngest son Johann Christian and from Haydn. But has one explained the living Mozart by referring to models? And in this first European of music, who with unprecedented universality ('inner Catholicity', if one understands the phrase correctly) had an intense interest in the whole musical environment of his

13

time and all the musical tradition at his disposal, one can find an amazing variety, differentiated yet balanced, of all the personal and regional styles and all the genres of the music of his time. One can identify and analyse 'German', 'French' or 'Italian', homophony and polyphony, learned music and galants, development and contrast. But do references to influences really explain the special character of Mozart's music?

Hardly. The new, unique feature, what I would say makes Mozart Mozart, does not consist of any kind of fused individual elements or prominent individual characteristics, but of the totality of the music. It lies in the totality of this music, its higher unity, rooted in the freedom of the spirit. What we have in the music is unmistakably Mozart himself. And that brings us round in a circle – though not a vicious circle: from the divinized Mozart back to Mozart the human being. But does that mean that if we do not want to speak of the divine Mozart, we should simply speak of the human Mozart and only of the human Mozart, the human being like you and me?

Theme 4:
The Human, All-too-human

It is to the credit of modern critical Mozart scholarship that it has done away with the quasi-religious, loaded 'devotion' to Mozart. It has rejected any even veiled ingratiation with the great hero and precisely in this way has brought out the human, all-too-human features of the apparently immaculate and unapproachable 'sun youth'. Since the 1950s, with spirit and forceful language Hildesheimer has made people generally aware of this demystification, which had already begun before him.[31] In fact, in the case of Mozart there is not just the usual difference between person and work, but there are undeniable 'contradictions between Mozart's life and his influence'.[32] Particularly at times of his highest creativity, Mozart took a remarkable and perhaps understandable delight in childlike and childish jokes, tomfoolery of all kinds, comic alliteration and other types of rhymes and not least in anal eroticism and scatology – something that has always been particularly painful for readers of Mozart's letters. Self-appointed posthumous Mozart psychiatrists who tend to take the playful wit and dexterity of south German talk so literally and with such Prussian earnestness regard this as the sign of an infantile-regressive personality. Just think how many chapters on Mozart would not have been written had that frivolous 'little cousin' not kept the letters of the twenty-year-old genius who was bubbling over to compensate![33]

However, the course of the history of Mozart reception from romantic divinization to a cool cutting him down to human size, from transcendent hero worship to dismissive 'little cousinification', from the hymns to Mozart to the largely unhistorical but nevertheless evocative film *Amadeus*, perhaps need yet further correction.[34] The principle holds that it is virtually impossible to deduce the musical characteristic of any of Mozart's works from contemporary events in his own life with any degree of certainty. Autobiographical causalities come to grief here. Nor may the 'minor clouds' in Mozart's life and work be turned into an ideology. One has only to hear how in the one G minor quintet, after only four beats, the muted espressivo in a pure diatonic E major begins to break apart and fragment in a chromatic mode which becomes increasingly intense ... More recent interpreters are certainly right when in the light of Mozart's life story they pay particular attention to the famous minor works and the dark minor passages in almost all his more large-scale instrumental compositions. They are right, as opposed to all the smooth harmonizers who think that Mozart's 'wretched and degraded earthly existence was, in the last analysis, fulfilled in the lofty realms of creativity', that 'his misery paid off, so to speak'.[35] Truly, Mozart found neither fulfilment nor a resting place, even in Vienna.

Nevertheless, the fact should not be suppressed that even in the face of mounting difficulties, Mozart's very last symphony – which Hildesheimer does not discuss – in shining C major has virtually no melancholy minor clouds. More than a difference of temperament may explain why Karl Barth does not follow Hildesheimer in praising the somewhat gloomy Serenade no. 12 in C minor (KV 388, 'Night Music'), but chooses instead the joyous Serenade no. 11 in E flat major (KV 375), and that along with the 'Jupiter' symphony he also praises *The Magic Flute* (according to Hildesheimer 'always overestimated'; indeed he criticizes it for misogyny[36]). In fact, the Protestant Barth once told me with great satisfaction in Basel that he had wanted Mozart's Coronation Mass to be performed at the World Council of Churches Assembly at Evanston. However, this evidently seemed far too ecumenical for the World Council of Churches. Just imagine, the performance of a Roman Catholic mass at the end of a Protestant world assembly! At any rate, Karl Barth, whose attitude became increasingly ecumenical as time went on, had surely noted that the Coronation Mass ends with an incomparable setting of the *Agnus Dei* with its '*Dona nobis pacem*'. Here is a prayer for peace, that peace which the churches constantly preach to the world but which they cannot achieve among themselves and for themselves, even after the fall of the Berlin wall and other walls (instead of a final abolition of excommunications there is only an agreement on a shared church tax). Could not the '*Dona nobis pacem*', brought to life in the spirit of Mozart, give a better direction for the churches today?

The question remains: has this brought us perhaps one step nearer to the phenomenon of Mozart? Can we now describe more closely the enigma of Mozart, the 'mystery' of the genius, even if we cannot decipher it?

Theme 5:
The Mystery

'Great music is always ambiguous.' So remarks a recent introduction to Mozart's instrumental music.[37] Yes – and no! For example, despite all the many dimensions of his music, one cannot find cacophony, randomness, total chaos in Mozart. However, there is one thing that one can find – through all the dynamics, expressive power, colour and variation, right down to the extremely controlled and clear writing in the scores even until the month of his death – and that is a mysterious order. No matter whether this music is performed nowadays on period instruments or in accordance with traditional, modern practice, the ordering of tones and sounds shows a 'sense of form' which Ferruccio Busoni had already called 'almost superhuman'.[38]

Both Hildesheimer and Barth, neither inclined to transfigure the one whom Busoni called the 'divine master', nor inclined to belittle Mozart as 'someone like you and me', speak of Mozart's 'mystery' which escapes any ultimate analysis or rational explanation.[39] Does this mystery perhaps lie only at an emotional level, or does it lie deeper?

It seems to me that Karl Barth's theological interpretation, which is primarily interested in Mozart's work, has come nearer to this mystery of Mozart's music than that of Hildesheimer, which is psychoanalytic and prefers to see

Mozart in terms more of Dionysius than of Apollo, who used to be his patron deity. We must start from the fact that the real Mozart:

as an infant prodigy was never really a child and in some respects remained childlike as an adult;

could be relaxed and cheerful, although in the end the harshness of the struggle for survival did not leave him much to laugh about;

from Paris onwards increasingly sided with Enlightenment criticism, though he showed no doubts about the Catholic faith and even after his stay in Paris immediately before the Revolution was neither an atheist nor an agnostic;

pressed onwards towards writing a new kind of music which very soon after his death was recognized as 'classical', although he did not see himself as a revolutionary.

And if we start from there, from the fact that this Mozart did not write divine music, nor demonic music either, but rather a music which was humane in every respect, then the mystery of this music lies in the fact that it constantly makes audible both the light *and* the dark, joy *and* sorrow, life *and* death. However, neither side stands neutrally in equilibrium over against the other and through the other, but the darkness is always transcended and done away with in the light.

In my view, here Barth may have hit on a decisive point: Mozart 'translated into music real life in all its discord. But in defiance of that, and on the sure foundation of God's good creation, and because of that, he moves always from left to right, never the reverse. This, no doubt, is what is meant by his triumphant "charm"' (though it should be noted that 'right' and 'left' are not meant in a political sense).[40] Or, to leave things less open to misunderstanding: 'A *turning* in which the light increases and the shadows fall,

19

though without disappearing, in which joy overtakes sorrow without extinguishing it, in which the Yes rings out louder than the ever-present No.'[41]

Barth thought that whenever one heard Mozart's music, one was 'transported to the threshold of a world which in sunlight and storm, by day and by night, is a good and ordered world. Then, as a human being of the twentieth century, [one] always finds oneself blessed with courage (not arrogance), with tempo (not an exaggerated tempo), with purity (not a wearisome purity), with peace (not a slothful peace).' Indeed, 'with an ear open to Mozart's dialectic', one 'can be young and become old, can work and rest, be content and sad: in short, one can live'.[42] That is the decisive thing: in Barth's interpretation of Mozart, as in Mozart himself, one hears 'the positive far more strongly than the negative'.[43]

Is all this just theological embellishment? Hardly, for others, too, have heard Mozart like this. Granted, one does not need to hear him like this, nor will one do so if one is tuned quite differently in one's own depths. Even Mozart's music can hardly communicate harmony and beauty to those who are mentally deranged or disturbed, nor can it make a hypochondriac smile, though the laughing Mozart in the end promised redemption even to Hermann Hesse's Steppenwolf. Indeed, there is mention in Steppenwolf of a 'golden divine trace'[44] which is often overgrown, a 'trace of God'[45] in this foolish-absurd human life. And this leads me to a further question. Does Mozart's music simply stem from some devotion to being or creation, or is it about something more? Does the mystery perhaps have an even deeper foundation?

Theme 6:
Bliss

It is clear that Mozart's music does not contain any message of faith as does that of Bach, nor is it a confession of life like that of Beethoven or Bruckner, far less programme music like that of Liszt or Wagner. Even in his operas, even in *The Magic Flute*, Mozart does not set out to teach or moralize. Think of all the things that people have read into his keys, above all E major and G minor – so often contradicting one another in the process; and the texts over which for a long time he did not always have a choice, particular though he was, were often lamentable enough. Mozart's primary concern was simply to make music, to make music with 'expression', using every possibility of melody and harmony. Music was his be-all and end all. Or was it really?

Even today, some Mozart interpreters cannot understand how after the deaths of his mother and his father Mozart could go back to the order of the day, to further compositions, relatively quickly. Is this just an easy-going attitude,[46] the pressure of deadlines, an obsession with music? Is it even the expression of a fatalism, as Hildesheimer remarked?[47] But was Mozart really a fatalist? And do his last three great symphonies demonstrate for the first time in the history of music a 'critical world view',[48] the expression even of an artist sickened by modernity?

Here I must once again take up, this time more in the

major, the theme which I initially treated in the minor, and go into that reality which in Mozart's view had not been understood by the cantor of the Thomaskirche, far less by Voltaire (whom he reviled with somewhat excessive vigour as a 'godless arch-rascal'[49]). This was the reality which in his view neither Protestant nor agnostic could understand in quite the same way: being Catholic. Being Catholic is not, however, to be understood as 'Catholicism', as an institution, as a church power characterized by dogmatism and moralism, for which Mozart did not in fact have the slightest understanding. Rather, it is a Catholicity which is by no means out of keeping with the gospel, rooted in a confident personal holding fast to God. 'Hold fast to God, I beg you, who will see to everything', the twenty-one-year old Wolfgang wrote to his father Leopold.[50] Here we have the expression of a religious conviction which comes to Catholics over the span of many centuries, and which they virtually take for granted. It is a belief in God, his providence and eternal life, which for Mozart need not constantly be striven for in a strictly Lutheran way, in a constant struggle with your conscience or through pangs of conscience. Indeed, it is a belief relatively immune even to modern criticism of religion, while at the same time being quite compatible with a religious scorn for clergy and church and in the long run even with humanistic Masonic ideals. All in all, it is a good Catholic assurance beyond all optimism and pessimism, an assurance – and now I quote – 'of things hoped for, the conviction of things not seen'. That is what we can read in the first verse of the eleventh chapter of the letter to the Hebrews, a description of faith which nowadays is endorsed by ecumenically-minded Catholics and Protestants alike.

That explains why Mozart, who was neither an Apollonian favourite of the gods nor a sad melancholic, hardly thought about the 'meaning of life', the 'task of human beings on the earth' – at least in the sources available to us.[51] Is this the expression of religious indifference? Certainly not. It is more an expression of what any Salzburg child as it were took for granted, an expression of a Catholic faith which had been communicated to the young Mozart above all by his father, who, while critical, nevertheless had a profound faith. For Leopold Mozart – who had been educated for twelve years by Jesuits and after a year studying theology became a baccalaureate in philosophy[52] – had brought up his young son as a Catholic, given him religious instruction, and in his letters to Paris had not hesitated to remind Wolfgang even as an adult to continue to practise his religion (by going to mass and making his confession). There is no doubt that Mozart's unquestioning faith, his holding fast to a meaning in life – on which he hardly reflected in theory – have their roots here. And this was expressed and responded to in a basic question in the catechism: 'Why is man created on earth?' Then as now, to some people this gives an answer for the whole of life: it may be sorely tried in the tribulations of that life, but is never seriously given up.

Of course there were also such catechisms in the time of Mozart. For example, the learned priest and educationalist Dr Ignaz Parhamer composed one in 1749 under the title 'Historical Catechism'.[53] And this Dr Parhamer was an old acquaintance of the Mozart family. He was the director of an orphanage which the Mozarts had visited on 12 September 1768 and in which Wolfgang Mozart, who was only twelve, was able to hear the performance of his first great mass, the famous 'Orphanage Mass' in C minor (KV 139), which he conducted himself, on 7 December 1768. However, the classical 'Christian Catholic Catechism for City and Country' by Peter Canisius may still have been wide-spread in Austria and probably even in Salzburg. Here the basic question why man was created was answered like this: 'To know, praise, worship, love and serve God and in this way to achieve eternal bliss.'[54]

So we can see how it is a sign of a deeply grounded belief in God and not an irreligious 'fatalism' for Mozart, apparently affected only superficially, to say that God brought about the deaths even of his mother and his father. For him these were no 'blows of fate' or shattering 'breaks in life' but a 'decree'. Certainly Mozart all too often uses the phrase 'my God', 'O God', merely as a thoughtless and empty form of expression – in a way which is sadly all too common everywhere, even now. He was as little concerned to define the concept of God as he was to define love. But why should he not have been in earnest when after the death of his mother in 1778 (on 3 July), he wrote to his father that he had been 'consoled' by his 'entire and steadfast submission to the will of God'?[55]

And why should he not have been in earnest when in 1787 (4 April), only four years before his own death, he wrote in a letter to his father, who was mortally ill: ' . . . I never lie down at night without reflecting that – young as I am – I may not live to see another day. Yet no one of all my acquaintances could say that in company I am morose and disgruntled. For this blessing I daily thank my Creator and wish with all my heart that each one of my fellow-creatures could enjoy it.'[56]

So to think that Mozart had little or no religious feeling, for example in the tremendous *Kyrie*, *Gloria* or *Sanctus* of the great fragmentary C Minor Mass, would not just go against the extraordinary musical quality and intensity of this music which subtly brings out the meaning of each

24

individual word. It would also go against the Catholic faith which he never denied, even if in his case this was also coloured by Freemasonry and the Enlightenment.

The degree to which beneath the surface Mozart lived by his Catholic faith emerges particularly clearly in the account of a conversation with the cantor of the Thomaskirche in Leipzig. Hildesheimer passed it over and Barth only apostrophized it. The cantor, Johann Friedrich Doles, was a pupil of Johann Sebastian Bach, and the conversation took place in 1789, two years before Mozart's death.[57] Mozart is said to have remarked that this 'enlightened Protestant' did not grasp what the *Agnus Dei qui tollis peccata mundi, dona nobis pacem*, etc., was all about. He then went on to speak of his own religious experience. 'But if someone has been introduced from earliest childhood, as I have been, into the mystical sanctuary of our religion; if there, when you did not yet know how to cope with your dark but urgent feelings, you waited for worship with an utterly fervent heart, without really knowing what you wanted, and went away with a lighter and uplifted heart without really knowing what you had had; if you thought how lucky were those who knelt down at the moving *Agnus Dei* and received the eucharist, and at the communion the music spoke in quiet joy from the hearts of those kneeling there, *Benedictus qui venit*, then it is all quite different.' This was Mozart's experience as a boy. And now? 'Now, though, that gets lost in the life of the world; but – at least that's the case with me – once you really take in again words which you have heard a thousand times, in order to set them to music, it all comes back. It stands before you, and moves your soul.' The 'mystical sanctuary of our religion', 'it all comes back', the movement of the 'soul' – is that language of someone who is not caught up into church music, who is not involved, someone without any 'creative expression of a confession of faith'?

Of course the sceptic can raise the question whether Mozart maintained this almost automatic confidence in his God and creator, in 'bliss', even when thinking of his own death, which was possible at any time, and in the 'mystical sanctuary of our religion' even in the last two months of his life. Think of the triumphant and at the same time unfathomable course from his infant pieces KV 1–3 to the painfully dissonant chromaticism and rhythmic harshness of the little Leipzig gigue in G major KV 574 of 1789 or the D major minuet KV 594a (355) of 1790! Given the lack of interest on the part of the Vienna public, spoilt by fashion, the disappearance of Mozart's hope of a suitable position at court, his financial difficulties and increasingly poor health, some biographers speak, not without reason, of a 'darkness surrounding Mozart's last months' which 'can hardly be cleared up now',[58] whereas others, in reaction, feel able to speak of a 'most creative and on the whole a successful and happy year'.[59] Gernot Gruber seems to me to be correct when he remarks: 'After a trough in the waves there could well have been a crest – there is a lot of evidence that in the autumn of 1791 Mozart could have looked forward hopefully to a successful future. However, his unexpected death gave the crisis of the previous years the appearance of being a fatal one.'[60]

If we look more closely at Mozart the believer, we can see that all the detective work of sceptical analysts can hardly discover anything really 'incriminating' here, material for a chronicle of scandal, even by using psychoanalytical methods. Nor need I become involved at this point in the great dispute between the critics of Constanze and those who support her. In any case we may conclude that someone who despaired of men and God, who had 'given up', would not have worked indefatigably to his very last days. In 1791, the year of his death, in addition to minuets, German dances, Ländler and Contredances he could not at the same time have composed the highly acclaimed *Magic Flute* and the coronation opera *The Clemency of Titus*; he could not have composed the *Ave verum*, the 'Short Masonic Cantata', the B flat major Piano Concerto, perhaps the gentlest of his concerti, and the Clarinet Concerto; he would not have sung some of his very last incomplete work, his *Requiem*, on his death bed the very evening before his unexpected death.

No, it was no 'un-Mozartean speculative self-appease-ment'[61] when Wolfgang Amadeus Mozart wrote in the same letter to his father: 'As death, when we come to consider it closely, is the true goal of our existence, I have formed during the last few years such close relations with this best and truest friend of mankind, that his image is not only no longer terrifying to me, but is indeed very soothing and consoling. And I thank my God for graciously granting me the opportunity (you know what I mean) of learning that death is the *key* which unlocks the door to our true happiness.'[62]

So here we have the reason for the statement: 'For this blessing I daily thank my Creator and wish with all my heart that each one of my fellow-creatures could enjoy it.' And I gratefully confess that thirty-five years ago, in a garret in Paris where there were only a dozen discs, just the Clarinet Concerto KV 622, this last orchestral work of Mozart's completed precisely two months before his death, of unsurpassable beauty, intensity and inwardness, completely without any traces of gloom or resignation, delighted, strengthened, consoled, and in short brought a touch of 'bliss' to a doctoral student in theology almost every day.

Any of you may at some time have felt such small moments of 'bliss' when listening to Mozart's music. And that brings me to my personal confession of Mozart.

Theme 7 and Finale:
Traces of Transcendence

It is not Mozart's mere existence or person, but his work which may preserve us from meaninglessness and despair. Of course you can hear Mozart's music in very different ways: as a musical Philistine, as a music lover or a musicologist; on the radio or on disc, or directly in the concert hall; with score in hand or as it were all ears, with your hand on your heart; scrupulously paying attention in fidelity to every detail of the notes and the work, or emotionally caught up into the miraculous world of sound hidden behind the notes. In the last resort the most important thing may be whether, in studying it or simply in sampling it, we open ourselves completely to this music, let it take us over, enter completely into it.

If we do this, we can experience that Mozart's music in particular is the lofty art of transcending, understood – primarily in musicological terms – as the art of exposition, variation and transition.[63] Indeed, even as a lay person one can be fascinated with many features of Mozart's music. One can see:

how all the musical genres are shaped and at the same time – in sonatas, chamber music, symphonies and especially in the operas – how their limits are transcended;

how in these genres styles change and run into one another – one need only think of the incorporation of features of Bach's counterpoint and the oratorios of Handel, or the C Minor Mass with the 'baroque' *Kyrie eleison* and the 'modern' *Christe eleison*;

how in the genres an inimitable balance is achieved between the contrasts – of D minor diatonic, chromatic, enharmonic – in a way which makes possible countless surprising transitions which have all the attraction of uncertainty as to where we are coming from and where we are going;

how in particular the adagio as the central movement between the dramatic and dance-like outer movements speaks a new language of the soul, often of a meditative kind: the new espressivo of the melody of humanity and the arias without words, which often assume the character of contemplation, of spiritualized love, of meditation and prayer.

And does this transcending of musical categories, of the bounds of genres and modes in the most subtle of all spiritual arts, have anything to do with transcendence in the real sense? Certainly. That is of course most obvious in Mozart's sacred music, which is not at all sentimental, but strong and moving. Happily it does not yet know the complete distinction made by the traditionalist church music reformers of the nineteenth century between secular and sacral art, yet it can distinguish very clearly between opera and church: for example where Mozart, the music dramatist *par excellence*, composes the transition from *passus et sepultus*, crucified and buried, to *resurrexit* and *ascendit*, rose and ascended, and achieves transcendence in the process. Is it just like the opera? Certainly not. 'It all sounds very well,' says Mozart of a mass of a well-known opera composer of the time, 'but not in church', and to make the point as far as the creed he gives the aforesaid mass an amusing secular text (for example, instead of the 'Kyrie eleison', 'Devil take it! He goes fast!').[64]

In his own mature works the theologically unconsidered but highly sensitive setting of the liturgical texts forms not only the space, the framework, the atmosphere for the liturgy, but is itself liturgy resounding in music. Of his more than sixty pieces of church music, one need think only of the C Minor Mass, the Credo Mass or the Coronation Mass, and also of the *Ave verum corpus* from the end of his life, which in the intense expressiveness of its melody and chromatic harmony can show how music itself can be worship. Mozart died on 5 December 1791 over his last, greatest but incomplete mass – in the middle of the movement *Lacrimosa dies illa . . .* [65]

But music is not finished even when it is written out, nor even when it is performed. For the listener, too, has an effect on it in each new context. The composition, presentation and reception of music (it is the same with literature and the graphic arts) form a complex linkage. In thus venturing to return from the process of composition to the process of hearing, I am not talking of what Mozart's genius must deliberately (or even programmatically) have set to music, but what the music of this genius (and every genius is gift, or better grace) can itself give us – though everything depends on the capacity of the hearer. So it is very important how one hears Mozart, and once again there are an enormous number of ways of interpreting his music and receiving it. No one has a monopoly of interpretation here, least of all the theologian, who must from the start be on guard against commandeering art for religion.

Yet even musical specialists would not dispute that the listener with a religious orientation also has a right to personal experiences of the music of this by no means unreligious musician, music in which spirit and form coincide, and which is perhaps able to say something which cannot be expressed in words, but only in sounds. And for all the academic and rational matter-of-factness of a preoccupation with the historically unique phenomenon of Mozart, it is this one experience which keeps drawing me to this music. If I try to surrender completely to Mozart's music, without outside disturbances, alone at home or at a concert, I suddenly feel how far I have got away from being confronted with the body of sound: I hear only the form of the music, music and nothing else. It is the music which completely surrounds me, permeates me and suddenly echoes from within. What has happened? I detect that I am directed completely inwards, with eyes and ears, body and spirit; the self is silent, and all external factors, all encounter, all the split between subject and object, has for a moment been overcome. The music is no longer something over against me, but is what embraces me, penetrates me, delights me from within, completely fulfils me. The statement comes to mind: 'In it we live and move and have our being.'

However, as we know, this is a scriptural phrase, taken from the speech of the apostle Paul on the Areopagus in Athens, where Paul is speaking of seeking, sensing and finding *God*, who is not remote from any of us, and in whom we live, move and have our being.[66] Not only would the agnostic Hildesheimer, who rejects any revelation, have found it rash to apply this saying from God's revelation to music, but also Barth the dogmatic theologian, who wanted to limit revelation completely to the word of the Bible and only towards the end of his life (in the last volume of his uncompleted *Church Dogmatics*) was prepared to recognize other lights, words and truths in the created world –

albeit, as he thought, only so to speak as reflections of that one light, as reflections of that one truth and revelation. For Barth it was no longer permissible to speak of music and even of Mozart in this connection.[67]

So am I fantasizing or speculating? No. 'When I hear great music, I believe that I know that what this music says cannot be untrue.'[68] So conceded the musicologist Theodor W. Adorno, who as is well known was more than reserved towards traditional religion. He was taking part in a discussion about revelation and autonomous reason. As an example Adorno gave Bach's *St Matthew Passion*; he could equally well have given Mozart's *Requiem*. I think that music which speaks the truth is not just limited, say, to vocal music or explicitly religious music; it also includes purely instrumental music – and especially the intimacy of many second movements. An abstract masterpiece can speak the truth in the pure language of sound. Indeed tones, sounds, can speak and in the end say something inexpressible, unspeakable: in the midst of music the 'ineffable mystery'.

Truly, more than any other music, Mozart's music – though it is not heavenly music but completely earthly music – seems to show in its sensual yet unsensual beauty, power and clarity, how wafer-thin is the boundary between music, which is the most abstract of all arts, and religion, which has always had a special connection with music. For both, though they are different, direct us to what is ultimately unspeakable, to mystery. And though music cannot become a religion of art, the art of music is the most spiritual of all symbols for that 'mystical sanctuary of our religion', the divine itself. In other words, for me Mozart's music has relevance for religion not only where religious and church themes or forms emerge, but precisely through the compositional technique of the non-vocal, purely instrumental music, through the way in which this music interprets the world, a way which transcends extra-musical conceptuality.

Certainly, one must be open to this music in a special manner, and here any interpretation moves in a tricky area. A critic has rightly said of theological interpretation: 'Mozart could also intend something quite diabolical with it (his music), a jest, a nihilism behind the appearance of tender understanding, a higher form of amorality.'[69] Indeed, Mozart's music is certainly no proof of God. But is it a proof of nihilism? There can certainly be no question of that.

On the contrary, there are countless men and women who can confirm that in certain moments of attunement a gift may be given to those sensitive people who are ready to hear, alone yet not alone, and to open themselves in that rational yet supra-rational trust of which I have spoken. With keen ears they may also perceive in the pure, utterly internalized sound, for example of the adagio of the Clarinet Concerto, which embraces us without using any words, something wholly other: the sound of the beautiful in its infinity, indeed the sound of an infinite which transcends us and for which 'beauty' is no description. So here are cyphers, traces of transcendence. One need not perceive them, but one can – there is no compulsion here. If I allow myself to be open, then precisely in this event of music which speaks without words I can be touched by an inexpressible, unspeakable mystery. In this overwhelming, liberating experience of music, which brings such bliss, I can myself trace, feel and experience the presence of a deepest depth or a highest height. Pure presence, silent joy, happiness. To describe such experience and revelation of transcendence religious language still needs the word God, the nature of which (according to Nicolas of Cusa) makes up that *coincidentia oppositorum*, the reconciliation of all opposites, which is also characteristic of Mozart's music.

But I shall stop there and not force anything on anyone. From the start I have not been concerned to commandeer this great music for religion. My concern has been with my own experiences *with* this music, which of course are shaped by my own life and faith. Someone might ask whether these experiences might not have ended up making me a fanatic, a Mozart fanatic or, even worse, a religious fanatic. But none of this has to do with mystical transports, madness or ecstasy, either in Mozart's case or mine. Even Bernard Shaw, that old scoffer, called Mozart's music 'the only music yet written that would not sound out of place in the mouth of God'.[70] So as an enlightened person at the end of the twentieth century I am not suddenly losing all reason when I listen to Mozart's music. Rather, my reason is being restored. Indeed, now and then I am transported to that peace which transcends all critical and even theological reason. For that I can never be grateful enough to Mozart, and such peace is something that I wish you all.

Opium of the People?

Theological Reflections on
Mozart's Coronation Mass

Does Mozart's music need long explanations? Hardly. The music of this incomparable composer is accessible to anyone who is open to it. It really does not need words.

So one can also listen to Mozart's *Missa Brevis* in C major (KV 317), as to Mozart's seventeen church sonatas for organ and orchestra – purely instrumental music from the same decade – without being 'bothered' by words.

And yet, this mass is not just a work for instruments; it is also a work with words. Here Mozart has set to music the texts of the Roman mass. They are fixed; they resisted all changes for a millennium, and from the fifteenth century at the latest stand at the centre of church music, being set polyphonically as a cycle. The *Kyrie*, *Gloria*, *Credo*, *Sanctus* and *Benedictus*, and *Agnus Dei* are five very different classical structural elements of the Catholic celebration of the eucharist.

Mozart was a composer of church music from a very early age. He was ten years old when he composed his first Kyrie (KV 33), and twelve when he wrote his first mass (KV 49), which was to be followed by seventeen others. He died while writing his last, greatest, but incomplete mass, his Requiem. The list of Mozart's works includes more than sixty pieces of church music – not forgetting the two

Vespers and four Litanies. Certainly his masses are anything but 'official music' at the periphery of his compositions.[71] But what are they? How are they to be interpreted? How is their effect to be described? Is music, church music, Mozart's music, opium of the people? Is that a permissible question?

The Horizon of the Time

Salzburg in the spring of 1779: Mozart was twenty-three when he composed this 'Coronation Mass'; his post Court and Cathedral Organist to the Prince Archbishop.[72] The title of the work is not his own; it was given to this mass because the occasion for its composition was thought to be the coronation of the statue of the Virgin in the pilgrimage church on Maria Plain or the coronation of Leopold II or Francis II. In all probability, however, this composition (completed on 23 March 1779) was intended for the Easter celebrations in Salzburg Cathedral. At any rate, that is where it received its first performance.

Salzburg 1779: we have to imagine a city and land ruled over by a typical representative of European feudalism who had been able to weld church and secular power into an omnipotent synthesis, in the paradoxical form of a prince archbishop. The present occupant of this archiepiscopal princely seat was a count who took a delight in reform, Hieronymus Colloredo.[73] And one result of his reforming zeal was what we would nowadays call liturgical reform. A mass was not to take long – not because of some unmusical whim of a prince of the church, but as a consequence of his enlightened pastoral concern. The aim was to guard against the excesses of church music, particularly as expressed in Italian virtuoso art with the help of castrati and prima donnas, and once again to find a place for church music within the liturgy. For a young court composer like Wolfgang Amadeus Mozart, this was a challenge: the requirement was extreme brevity and a concentrated form. 'So you see a special study is required for this kind of composition,' Mozart had written to Fr Giambattista Martini,[74] one of the leading Italian musical theorists. This was the comment of someone born in Salzburg, who as is well known had made an indefatigable study of all styles and genres of music and therefore had also studied the church music of Haydn, Richter, Wagenseil, the Italians and the French, learning from all and succumbing to none. It was the comment of someone who, endowed with a fantastic musical memory, had applied himself in a quite personal way. The result, moreover, is the mass with which we are concerned, the 'Missa Brevis' in C major' – a 'short mass'.

When the mass is the subject of a composition, presuppositions and inherent features need to be taken account of. The basis is provided by the words of the liturgical text. Mozart left these untouched. He allowed himself no textual omissions of the kind that were frequent at the time and were later resorted to by Franz Schubert, who in the creed strikingly always omitted the line about the 'one holy catholic and apostolic church' (and on occasion other parts as well). The result was a work whose words were eminently understandable. Moreover, the compositional technique was not just mechanically to bring together individual particles, in the way that later led to criticism of the 'Mozart-Haydn school' from Romantics like Robert Schumann. No, here is a work with a classical unity: stylistically it is held together not only by the basic key of C major, which persists almost throughout with very rare modulations, but also by the combination of choir and orchestra. The first part of the *Kyrie eleison* is repeated with variations after the central *Christe eleison*; the *Credo* is in rondo form, and finally the andante of the *Kyrie* recurs once again at the end, in the *Agnus Dei*. All these are deliberate features of the composition, which give the whole work a well-planned unity.

Prince Archbishop Hieronymus Colloredo was certainly a zealot for reform, but he was also a harsh man who ruled – when necessary – with brutality. He was an autocrat in the soutane of a bishop. Two years before this mass Mozart had asked for his release from the archbishop – in order to move from narrow, clerical Salzburg, which he so disliked, to Paris. As a result his father was also dismissed from archepiscopal service as a court musician. In a letter to his father on the journey to Paris, Wolfgang speaks quite bluntly: 'Always remember, as we do, that our Mufti H(ieronymus) C(olloredo) is an idiot, but that God is compassionate, merciful and loving.'[75] On arrival in Paris, the twenty-year-old Wolfgang, accompanied by his mother, sought a new fortune as an artist, but despite some fine compositions (*Les petits riens*, flute concerti, the Paris symphony, and the A major sonata) had no success. On the contrary, the Paris journey ended in catastrophe, since the following summer (on 3 July 1778) Mozart's mother died.

Paris was the city of Louis XVI and Marie Antoinette (whom the infant prodigy Wolfgang knew from Vienna), but also the city of Voltaire. This was the time when the critical, individualistic spirit of the Enlightenment increasingly came into conflict with the feudalism and absolutism of church and state. That same year, 1778, Voltaire had been buried – having been refused a Christian funeral! So in Paris Mozart was in an atmosphere which was

43

increasingly fraught with conflict and increasingly tense. Did the allegedly unpolitical Wolfgang, who could mock priests and monks and yet later became a freemason, suspect that this Ancien Régime, this alliance of throne and altar, which was scorned by Voltaire and the men of the Enlightenment, was on its way to destruction while at the French court, fully secularized and yet 'Catholic', he was attending silent masses with concert accompaniments (organ music or great motets)? Did he hear the saying of Voltaire's which was being bandied around Paris, 'Écrasez l'infame', 'Destroy the infamous one' – of course aimed at the Catholic church? Did this Mozart, with so little of a revolutionary bent and with his mind completely on music, guess that the Archbishop Count Colloredo whom he hated so much, against whom he was to become a 'revolutionary' for the sake of his civic and artistic independence, would turn out to be the last ruling clerical prince of Salzburg? At all events the archbishop had no inkling of this.

The modern age had also cast its shadow forward at a very early stage in Austria, whither, at the wish of his father, Mozart had returned in 1779 to the 'slavery' of Salzburg. It appeared in the reforms of the emperor Joseph II, the enlightened 'crowned revolutionary' – after the death of Maria Theresia in 1780. Under Joseph II the bodyguard was abolished, a patent of tolerance was decreed for the Jews, and around 700 religious houses were secularized and abolished. As Mozart had to recognize, hardly any of this was favourable to the dissemination and publication of pure organ compositions.

A time of epoch-making revolution was in the making. In terms of social history Mozart's own influence amounted to a change from the commissioned music of the old musicians from Bach to Haydn, who had been dependent on the local ruler, to the music of independent bourgeois artists like Beethoven and Schubert.

Why am I relating all this? Because anyone who hears the Coronation Mass today should not forget the rumbling of thunder, the stormclouds which were gathering over the time and which broke in 1789 in Paris in the great revolution. The throne was swept away, and in the long run the altar was shattered. The modern view of the state and society made headway against the mediaeval feudalistic church. So the *Missa Brevis* is church music ten years before the volcano was to erupt in Paris with the French Revolution and the proclamation of the Universal Rights of Man. Once we are aware of the grumbling of this thunder, of the abyss into which this age was soon to fall – we can also hear in a different way the powerful C major *Kyrie* of this mass – 'Lord have mercy upon us!'.

The Kyrie

Indeed, once Mozart no longer had any obligations to the Salzburg 'Beggars' Court', he could coax out quite different sounds for the *Kyrie*. The demand for 'lightness' which Archbishop Colloredo could still put to his court composers in the light-hearted rococo period was soon no longer in place. Since more serious times were in view, also for him personally, Mozart, who all his life struggled for a good style in church music, wrote a different kind of church music and produced more serious tones – a year later the darkly solemn 'Munich Kyrie' in D minor (KV 341) and then above all that mighty torso of the C Minor Mass (KV 427) which, had Mozart been able to complete it, would have taken its place between Bach's B Minor Mass and Beethoven's *Missa Solemnis*. But in 1791, two years after the outbreak of the Revolution, Wolfgang Amadeus Mozart died.

The *Kyrie*, 'Lord, have mercy', is an age-old cry of Christianity. Originally in antiquity a cry of homage to a ruler or god, in Christianity it had become the call of the community to Christ and a litany, and in Rome in the year AD 50 had supplanted the intercessions which were customary there.[76] Here in the Coronation Mass it is and remains the expression of a childlike, unconditional trust in God's mercy. Indeed, with his eyes on God and Jesus Christ Mozart wrote a deeply confident, assured music which, if thought of as Easter music, can even radiate an almost triumphal certainty of victory. This brief, powerful, festive *Kyrie* is an expression of Mozart's own Christian faith, certainly coloured by the Enlightenment and yet held quite naturally. Granted, Mozart was not a religious thinker or a theological brain; he was anything but a pious fanatic and he was certainly not a saint in private life. Yet authentic faith is a 'secret cornerstone' for anyone who writes such music.[77] Moreover this *Kyrie* is also the expression of a glad, joyful certainty: 'Lord, have mercy! Yes, Lord, indeed you have mercy!'

Kyrie eleison.	*Lord, have mercy.*
Kyrie eleison.	*Lord, have mercy.*
Kyrie Eleison.	*Lord, have mercy.*
Christe eleison.	*Christ, have mercy.*
Christe eleison.	*Christ, have mercy.*
Christe eleison.	*Christ, have mercy.*
Kyrie eleison.	*Lord, have mercy.*
Kyrie eleison.	*Lord, have mercy.*
Kyrie eleison.	*Lord, have mercy.*

The Gloria

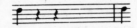

The *Kyrie* is followed by the *Gloria*, a Christian prayer of praise and petition like a psalm; originally it was the only real hymn in the mass. Composed in the Eastern Mediterranean in the fourth century, it was originally a hymn of thanksgiving and celebration, but in the West from the sixth century it was already part of the eucharist. Made up of three elements, it forms a synthesis of Jewish and Christian spirituality. There is the angels' song of praise on Christmas night ('Glory to God in the highest'), the praise of the one God rooted in the Hebrew Bible and then shaped by the New Testament ('*Benedicimus te*, we praise thee . . . '), and finally there are the petitions to Christ, the Lord and only Son of the Father ('*Domine, fili unigenite*, O Lord, the only begotten Son'). This is no triadic and trinitarian hymn but from earliest times an equally widespread binitarian hymn to God and his Son. In Mozart it becomes a blazing hymn of jubilant adoration with a uniquely uniform harmony, with no striving for effects or baroque self-indulgence.

My question is: is all this still 'church style'? Is not all this purely secular music, hardly to be distinguished from opera music (opera seria or opera sinfonia)? Is not this music utterly un-churchly and unliturgical, particularly if we compare it with Gregorian chant or the music of Palestrina? At any rate that was a widespread view of church musicians in the nineteenth century when the French abbot Dom Guéranger championed what was allegedly ancient Roman Gregorian chant as the only church ideal and thus as the universal norm of church music. In Germany Franz Xaver Witt, the church music reformer who in 1867 founded the Universal German Cecilia Association, and was also indebted to Romanticism, doubtless thought the same thing. For him (as also for H. Kretzschmar) Mozart's masses were a witness to 'decay in church music'. In the case of the Coronation Mass, from which one or two passages appear again later in operas, Witt could fume over the 'use of an opera in church consisting of sheer immoralities, which are depicted simply by the sensuous atmosphere of the music'.[78] But those anti-Enlightenment representatives of nineteenth-century liturgical conservatism, the neo-Gregorians who were akin to the neo-Gothics, neo-Romantics and neo-Scholastics, who now divinized tradition instead of reason and wanted to have a sharp division between sacred and profane music, either did not know or did not want to know that there is no one style of church music.

Were not some mediaeval church Gregorian melodies originally secular songs, even love songs? Were not some settings of the mass derived from dances or martial songs? And what about the organ, which purist Cecilians still allowed in church (without an orchestra)? In the Middle Ages, Renaissance and baroque period was it not a thoroughly secular, extremely popular instrument for accompanying dance music as well? And what about the great church musician Johann Sebastian Bach? Did not he, like Mozart, reject a fundamental division between secular and spiritual music, so that he could without hesitation use, for example, music from the secular birthday cantata

'Hercules at the Crossroads' for his Christmas Oratorio? What about that *a capella* art of Palestrina and the old classical vocal polyphony which rejected even organ accompaniment and which now in the perpetual change of musical style persists in a fossilized form as the 'embodiment of the old style'?[79] Is it really so different to present-day ears from the secular madrigal music of the time? No, this allegedly exemplary sixteenth-century church music was at any rate no less time-conditioned than that of Mozart, whose Salzburg type of mass found its most perfect expression in the Coronation Mass. There is no one style in church music. A division between sacred and secular music is unhistorical.

'Glory to God in the highest': is a greater contrast imaginable than that between this text, this music, and the life of the person who composed it? Is there a greater contrast than that between the master who is here already the 'unrivalled master of beauty in music'[80] and his treatment by this autocratic archbishop? In 1781, when Mozart petitioned for his release, he was reviled by the archbishop as a 'scoundrel, rogue and fox' and literally kicked out of the audience chamber by the archbishop's Master of the Kitchen, Count Arco, his three petitions for release having gone unanswered. Mozart was treated like a troublesome dog, dishonoured by the true masters 'in the highest' who claimed all 'glory' for themselves. But providence set things right. Mozart's prince of the church, who was expelled from his archbishopric in 1800 by the French and thus brought down in the world, had to witness the rise of his former organist and concert-master to world fame. He did not die until 1812, more than twenty years after Mozart. What will have gone through this Count's mind when he saw just whom he had treated like a servant? For after all, he had summoned his court composer to Vienna and in his house there had put him among the court servants. With an increasingly aroused sense of bourgeois status he had forbidden the budding genius of a composer to give public concerts at all, even charity concerts. And with all the arrogance of absolutist feudal power, he had virtually provoked the attempt of his concert-master to leave and the final break. 'I want to hear nothing more about Salzburg,' Mozart had written to his father at the time, 'I hate the archbishop to madness.'[81]

Yet all that princely clerical repression came to an end a few years later, when revolution broke out in Paris and heads rolled. There was no longer talk of '*Gloria in excelsis Deo*', then. Nor was there any longer talk of '*Pax, Pax, Pax*' (hammered home with great emphasis three times in the Coronation Mass), of 'peace among men with whom he is well pleased'! Glory to God? It was not least this feudal arrogance of power, unfortunately also practised by many representatives of the church, which caused the slogan 'Priests to the lantern' to go round Paris. Many people were now opposed to any belief in God, because it served the princes, bishops and priests ruling by the grace of God as a means of preventing the spread of the light of reason and keeping people in tutelage and slavery. Atheism became a political programme for the first time in world history. On 10 November 1793 the Christian God, to whom the *Gloria* had still been sung a dozen or so years earlier in the Coronation Mass, was deposed in Notre Dame in Paris and atheistic Reason was proclaimed as a rival goddess. Glory was now sung to Reason and the nationalistic state which embodied her, and in the name of the Fatherland the call quite consistently went out to great nationalistic wars: 'Allons, enfants de la Patrie.' The *Gloria* was replaced by the Marseillaise.

Down to our days – one might think of South American dictators or Franco's Spain – the church has been and is the support of an unsocial, corrupt and bankrupt 'ancien regime'. But have we learned the historical lessons? As Christians we know today that one must no longer protest against 'Freedom, Equality and Fraternity', the slogan at that time chiselled into all the churches in France, when we again sing the *Gloria in excelsis Deo*. Today we must no longer attack reason and justice, science and democracy, if we want to adopt the cause of God's peace among humankind. Realistic humanity is also possible today – supported by a rational trust in God. And is not that precisely what this *Gloria* ultimately seeks to express? The joy of Mozart's *Gloria* is first expressed in the forward movement of rapid triple time, 'We praise thee, we bless thee, we worship thee, we glorify thee, we give thee thanks.' But this joy in calling on Jesus, the one Lord among all the lords of this world, changes into the minor the moment that there is mention of the forgiveness of sins and mercy. This shows that contrary to all the optimism of the century Mozart – who at the age of fourteen had written out from memory the music of Allegri's famous *Miserere*, sung in the Sistine Chapel, the notes of which could not be either copied or lent out on pain of punishment from the church – gave realistic expression to that decisive dimension of being human associated with failure and incurring guilt.

Gloria in excelsis Deo	*Glory be to God on high*
et in terra pax	*and in earth peace*
hominibus bonae voluntatis.	*to men of good will.*
Laudamus te,	*We praise thee,*

benedicimus te,	we bless thee,
adoramus te,	we worship thee,
glorificamus te.	we glorify thee.
Gratias agimus tibi	We give thanks to thee
propter magnam	for thy great
gloriam tuam,	glory,
Domine Deus,	O Lord God,
Rex caelestis,	Heavenly King,
Deus Pater,	God the Father
omnipotens.	almighty.
Domine fili unigenite,	O Lord, the only-begotten Son,
Jesu Christe,	Jesus Christ,
Domine Deus, Agnus Dei,	Lord God, Lamb of God,
Filius Patris,	Son of the Father,
qui tollis	Thou that takest away
peccata mundi	the sins of the world,
miserere nobis;	have mercy upon us;
qui tollis	thou that takest away
peccata mundi,	the sins of the world,
suscipe deprecationem nostram.	receive our prayer.
Qui sedes	Thou that sittest
ad dexteram Patris,	at the right hand of the Father,
miserere nobis.	have mercy upon us.
Quoniam tu	For thou
solus sanctus,	only art holy,
tu solus Dominus,	thou only art the Lord,
tu solus Altissimus,	thou only art Most High,
Jesu Christe,	Jesus Christ
cum Sancto Spiritu:	with the Holy Spirit,
in gloria Dei Patris.	in the glory of God the Father.
Amen.	Amen.

'Glory to God in the highest and in earth peace, peace, peace to men.' What does the combination of music and faith look in this music of Mozart's? Mozart's mass was not a message of faith like the masses and cantatas of Johann Sebastian Bach or the oratorios of George Frederick Handel. Nor, however, was it devotional music experienced in a pious subjective way, in the style of Schubert. Far less was it romantic, deliberately personal confessional music in the style of Bruckner. Rather, this mass, composed in a universal tonal language, is the work of someone averse to all bigotry, who as a matter of course lives by the certainty of grace, by an Enlightenment Catholic piety which is to be compared with the light early baroque and rococo churches in which his music was performed. But what we have here is not just music *at* worship but music *of* worship: 'an exegesis of liturgy'. Mozart's ideals of piety and music were different from the ideals of those who preceded him and came after him. In its own particular perfection his setting of the mass texts in particular provides more than a spiritually attractive space for worship, a solemn and at the same time encouraging framework and a pious festal atmosphere. No, this music is the liturgy itself, ringing out in festal sound, and it gives musical expression to the subject matter, the liturgical text itself. So all in all this is liturgical music which expounds the text, and in its beauty, purity and perfection it already gives us a glimpse of the eternal, joyful sound of the spheres with their eternal Glorias: the *vita venturi saeculi*, the 'life of the world to come', which is confessed at the end of the *Credo*.

The Credo

Credo in unum Deum,
Patrem omnipotentem,
factorem caeli et terrae,
visibilium omnium
et invisibilium.
Et in unum dominum
Jesu Christum,
Filium Dei unigenitum,

et ex Patre natum
ante omnia saecula
Deum de Deo,
lumen de lumine,
Deum verum de Deo vero,
genitum, non factum,
consubstantialem Patri;

per quem omnia facta sunt.

Qui propter nos homines
et propter nostram salutem
descendit de caelis.
Et incarnatus est
de Spiritu Sancto

I believe in one God
the Father almighty,
maker of heaven and earth,
of all things visible
and invisible.
And in one Lord
Jesus Christ
the only-begotten Son of God,

begotten of his Father
before all worlds,
God of God,
Light of Light,
very God of very God,
begotten, not made,
of one substance with the Father,

by whom all things were made.

Who for us men
and for our salvation
came down from heaven,
and was incarnate
by the Holy Ghost

ex Maria Virgine,	of the Virgin Mary,
et homo factus est.	and was made man.
Crucifixus etiam pro nobis	And was crucified also for us
sub Pontio Pilato;	under Pontius Pilate;
passus	he suffered
et sepultus est.	and was buried.
Et resurrexit tertia die,	And the third day he rose again
secundum Scripturas,	according to the scriptures,
et ascendit	and ascended
in caelum,	into heaven,
sedet ad dexteram Patris.	and sitteth at the right hand of the Father.
Et iterum venturus est	And he shall come again
cum gloria,	with glory
iudicare vivos	to judge the living
et mortuos,	and the dead,
cuius regni	whose kingdom
non erit finis.	shall have no end.
Et	And I believe
in Spiritum Sanctum,	in the Holy Ghost,
Dominum et vivificantem:	the Lord and Giver of life,
qui cum Patre	who with the Father
et Filio	and the Son
simul adoratur	is worshipped
et conglorificatur:	and glorified;
qui locutus est	who spake
per prophetas.	by the prophets.
Et unam, sanctam,	And I believe one holy
catholicam	catholic
et apostolicam Ecclesiam.	and apostolic church.
Confiteor unum baptisma	I acknowledge one baptism
in remissionem peccatorum.	for the remission of sins.

Et expecto	*And I look for*
resurrectionem mortuorum	*the resurrection of the dead*
et vitam	*and the life*
venturi saeculi.	*of the world to come.*
Amen.	*Amen.*

The *Credo*, that confession of faith initially used at baptism, was first incorporated from the Eastern liturgy into the Spanish and Frankish mass (in the form laid down by the Councils of Nicaea and Constantinople) and from there after 1000 incorporated into the Roman mass. Since then it has been part of regular worship on Sundays and festivals. Musically, the *Credo* is not a hymn, like the *Gloria*, but a confession.

So the *Credo* of the Coronation Mass, too, begins with a powerful confession of the one God which is repeated at the end, ostinato, in the middle of the closing fugue on the Amen. Thus passages of festal solemnity and sensitive poetry contrast, yet remain in balance, in this longest and fullest of songs. For here more than ever, Mozart, the musician, who – according to a well-known saying of F. Grillparzer's – 'never did too little and never too much, who always achieved his goal and never went beyond it', as a born dramatist shaped the music by the text, which develops in trinitarian form over three parts. First comes the confession of the almighty God and Father, the creator of heaven and earth; then the confession of the one Lord Jesus Christ, the Son and the incarnate, crucified and risen. Finally comes the confession of the life-giving Holy Spirit. The only point of repose in this divine drama, unusually impressive and brought out by a solo quartet, is the message of the incarnation: 'and was made man'. Surprisingly, it leads into the deepest minor, in the powerful chorus '*Et crucifixus*', then to be followed by the message of the resurrection in a radiant C major.

So at the centre and turning point of the *Credo* – composed tenderly and almost shyly – stands the message of the Son of God incarnate. For Mozart, belief in Jesus as Son of God was certainly not a theological problem. But is that the case today? There is no mistaking the fact that for countless people – including those who hear Mozart's setting of the *Credo* – belief in Jesus as the Son of God incarnate is something which they can no longer accept. It sounds too much like ideology, illusion, projection.

Did not Ludwig Feuerbach,[82] the ex-theologian, who radicalized the French Enlightenment, demonstrate once for all in the middle of the nineteenth century what lies behind belief in the incarnate Son of God? Is not this simply belief in man made God? Indeed, the historical conflict between the Christian and the modern citizen, which in the case of the composer Mozart could still be worked out without fatal damage to his piety, was in the case of Feuerbach two generations later to end in atheism: atheism as the apparently true humanism. For that is the creed of Feuerbach which was accepted by many people in the nineteenth century: belief in man instead of belief in God; belief in a divinization of man instead of belief in the incarnation of God. The concept of God is no more than a human projection throwing up an illusion, the divine, which is the universally human projected on the beyond. That is how Feuerbach saw the future. 'Unbelief has taken the place of belief, reason the place of the Bible, politics the place of religion and the church, the earth the place of heaven, work the place of prayer, material need the place of hell, and man the place of the Christian.'

We must also keep this at the back of our minds when we

hear the Christian *Credo* today; no faith today can by-pass the criticism of religion. No faith is exempt from facing radically the suspicion of projection. There can be no faith which has not applied the instrument of religious criticism radically to itself. And yet we know today that the modern transvaluation of all values has not preserved human beings from inhumanity and barbarism, and that the prophesied 'downfall of Christianity' has not taken place. Even the projection argument seems to have been seen through, since a person's projection, as is true of all human faith, hope and love, can in reality nevertheless correspond to something real, namely God's reality. No, the Enlightenment optimism of Feuerbach, that belief in God itself would also disappear with an analysis of projections of God, is today itself an illusion: '*Credo in unum deum.*'

And yet, no theologian can disguise the fact that there is hardly a word in this *Credo* – from the word 'God' to statements about the virgin birth, descent into hell, ascension and eternal life – that does not need critical translation into present-day thought and present-day language. Certainly here we have a hallowed liturgical text which should not be abolished. But every word needs to be understood afresh.

The Sanctus

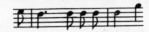

That applies not only to the *Credo* but also to the fourth structural element of the order of the Roman mass, which contains the oldest and most solemn biblical text of all, the 'thrice holy', the Trisagion of the seraphim which the prophet Isaiah heard in the vision at his call (Isaiah 6.3): 'Holy, holy, holy . . .'. Mozart gives the *Sanctus* wholly to a choir, i.e. to the community. Possibly on the model of Jewish worship (Kedosha) the 'thrice-holy' or Trisagion was incorporated into the liturgical prayer of the church at a very early stage and, from the fifth century on, with a preface formed the first part of the eucharistic prayer.

The new liturgical translation of '*Dominus Deus Sabaoth*' already shows the need for an interpretation for today. Nowadays the liturgy no longer has 'Lord God of Hosts', but 'God of power and might'. For the prophets of the Old Testament, too, this thrice-holy God is also the invisible God. In the temple Isaiah could see only the hem of his garment. But the focus of early Christianity is no longer on the Jerusalem Temple (which in the meantime had been destroyed) and the Holy of Holies there, but on the cosmos, which as a whole bears witness to God's unapproachable exaltation. So what we have here is a disclosure of God's hidden holiness – in his glory which appears in the world. Hence the words of the *Sanctus*: 'Heaven and earth are full of thy glory.'

Could a composer have failed to give this passage especially a triumphant musical form by setting it forte with a tutti bringing in all the choir and orchestra? After all, this is the most solemn moment in the mass, immediately before the account of the institution of the Lord's Supper: 'This is my body . . . this is my blood.' Timelessly great, indeed radiating over all creation, here God's exalted majesty is worshipped with the age-old cry of joy, 'Hosanna, Hosanna in the highest.' In Mozart there is a great andante maestoso, related to the *Kyrie* in its punctuated rhythm. But what about belief in God's majesty? Is that still possible today?

Certainly the baptized Jew Karl Marx,[83] the most significant pupil of Feuerbach in matters of religious criticism, knew the Trisagion. But he no longer believed that heaven and earth were full of God's glory. Rather, he proclaimed that the criticism of religion made by Feuerbach had to lead on to criticism of the contradictions of society and thus finally to practical revolution. 'The criticism of heaven' had to turn 'into the criticism of earth': 'the criticism of religion into the criticism of law, the criticism of theology into the criticism of politics.' Religion, not least in the seductive form of music, is 'opium of the people'. Now, instead of 'Hosanna in the Highest', revolutionary fanfares were to resound from the depths: 'The criticism of religion ends with the doctrine that man is the highest being for men, in other words with the categorical imperative to overthrow all conditions in which man is a humiliated, enslaved, abandoned, contemptible being.'

Certainly religion was all too often the opium of the people, and music, too – not only music to march to but also church music – can befog, bewitch and mislead. Many Christians are in danger of using musical solemnity to ward off the 'outside world', of lulling themselves into a world of religious feeling which can also be produced by music, and thus failing to take note of the practical problems of the time. Hence religion and music as the opium of the people. Who could overlook the fact that the church hierarchy, too, is often enough in danger of celebrating only itself with solemn masses, and confusing the triumph of the grace of God with its own triumph?

Conversely, however, we also have to learn that not only religion but also revolution can be the opium of the people, and that revolution, too, is all too often supported by music. And even Marx's anti-religious socialist society has not brought heaven on earth to a single people on this planet. So more than ever today people in East and West are asking whether we would really get on better on earth if the heavens were darkened. At any rate the great ideologies of the modern world, both revolutionary socialism and evolutionary technological progress, have meanwhile gone bankrupt and proved to be quasi-religions. And some people are beginning to understand that we might do better to sing 'Great God, we praise thee' to the one true God, the Lord of all power and might, to the one thrice-holy God, rather than to the eternal, almighty, all-wise God of progress:

Sanctus, Sanctus, Sanctus:	*Holy, holy, holy:*
Dominus Deus	*Lord God*
Sabaoth.	*of Hosts.*
Pleni sunt caeli	*Full are heaven*
et terra	*and earth*
gloria tua.	*of your glory.*
Hosanna in excelsis.	*Hosanna in the highest.*

Here, of course, the all-important thing is that this one true God should not again be imagined under the false mask of a neo-feudalist or absolutist secular or spiritual authority, but that he should show himself with his original face of loving-kindness. According to the whole of the New Testament he has revealed this true face in Jesus of Nazareth, who in his whole being, speaking and action is the image of God. Jesus is God's word, which has assumed human form. He is the anointed one, the Messiah, who comes in the name of the Lord. 'Blessed is he who comes in the name of the Lord', '*Benedictus qui venit in nomine Domini*'.

The *Benedictus*: it makes good theological sense that since the liturgical reform of the Second Vatican Council the *Sanctus* and *Benedictus* which have been customary in worship since the fifth century and originally formed a unity, separated only for programmatic reasons, should as far as possible again be prayed or sung as a combined song of praise. Why? Because God and the one whom he has sent belong together. Anyone who knows the Son also knows the Father. Mozart set this hymn to the Messiah to such a miraculously tender, relaxed and sensitive cantabile allegretto solo quartet that the loving-kindness and mercy of the one who is praised could hardly have been expressed more beautifully. So there is Hosanna at the end of the *Benedictus* also to him – the Hosanna musically recapitulated in an impressive unity with the *Sanctus* – Hosanna to him who comes in the name of the Lord. The solo quartet of the one to come is even allowed to interrupt the powerful chorus of the Hosanna once again.

After all that we have heard, can there still be any doubt about it? Anyone who has so well-planned a conception and carries it out so thoughtfully, who is able to transform the text without apparent effort, purely into music, also has a theological understanding of what it is about. Indeed, for him church music is not just a 'compulsory commission' but an 'affair of the heart'.[84] It is because of this evocative religious expressiveness in Mozart's music that it is still performed in services even today – in contrast to, say, the bravura Italian church music of the same century, above all the masses of the great Neopolitan Alessandro Scarlatti. Mozart succeeded more than any one else in this period in addressing our artistic-musical and liturgical-religious sensibility over time. His church music is characterized by a 'joyful depth from above'.

However, we may miss a reference to the suffering and dying Christ in the *Benedictus*. Nevertheless, this hymn of joy is in no way Dionysian in its marked yet delicate rhythm. Mozart, whose character, talent and musical execution was neither 'Apollonian nor demonic', would in no way have been able to play off Dionysus against the crucified one, as the pastor's son Friedrich Nietzsche did at a later stage,[85] having in his youth already failed to discover any God of loving-kindness. For behind Nietzsche's Dionysian dithyrambs and their hate-love of the highly moral and jealous executioner God who is hostile to life lie his bitter experiences of real Christianity. Faced with the Christ of this Christianity, he felt that he had to identify himself with the God Dionysus who suffered infinitely and yet kept rising again, thus justifying life with all its contradictions.

And indeed, what if 'God' were only the counter-concept to life? What if the concept of the 'beyond' were invented in order to devalue this earthly world? What if the concept of soul or spirit merely served to put the body in contempt; if the salvation of the soul were only to be obtained in a crazy circle between the rigours of penitence and the hysteria of redemption? What if self-destruction were made a mark, a 'duty', 'holiness', the 'divine' in human beings? What if finally the concept of the 'good man' supported all weaklings, ill-advised people who suffered at their own hands, over against the strong man who said yes, who was certain of the future and vouched for it? If all this were Christian morality and dogmatics, then indeed one would have to be with 'Dionysus against the crucified'. In that case one could no longer be Christ, but only anti-Christ.

However, despite all the ambivalence of Christianity as it really exists in history, in the light of the real Christ of history things may not be seen in this light. *Ecce homo!* In the light of this one person one cannot be Christian without being human. One cannot be Christian at the expense of being human; one cannot be Christian alongside, above or below being human; one must be Christian as a radical, truly human, way of being human. It is this which becomes possible in the light of the one who is praised so highly. For 'the goodness, the *philanthropia*, the loving kindness, of God our saviour has appeared' (Titus 3.4). Yes indeed, blessed, *benedictus*, is the one who comes in the name of the Lord.

Benedictus   *Blessed is he*
qui venit   *that cometh*
in nomine Domini.   *in the name of the Lord.*
Hosanna in excelsis.   *Hosanna in excelsis.*

Yet, human life also includes the experience of negativity, and that means not only suffering, sickness and death but also guilt and sin. And with guilt and sin is associated that symbol 'which takes away the sin of the world', the 'Lamb of God' who suffers in our place. 'Lamb of God' is a title for Jesus, as is that of the servant of God who suffers for others. And so after the *Benedictus*, it is consistent that there should be the petition, the *Agnus Dei*.

The Agnus Dei

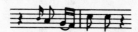

Agnus Dei,	*O Lamb of God,*
qui tollis	*that takest away*
peccata mundi,	*the sins of the world,*
miserere nobis.	*have mercy upon us.*
Agnus Dei,	*O Lamb of God,*
qui tollis	*that takest away*
peccata mundi,	*the sins of the world,*
miserere nobis.	*have mercy upon us.*
Agnus Dei,	*O Lamb of God,*
qui tollis	*that takest away*
peccata mundi,	*the sins of the world,*
dona nobis pacem.	*grant us thy peace.*

The song to Christ, the Lamb, was incorporated into the Roman liturgy from the Eastern liturgy, probably in the seventh century. Originally it had been sung as a litany during the breaking of the eucharistic bread for the faithful, which used to take a long time. The sacrificed lamb corresponded to the body of the Lord which was broken for us and given for us. So both great images interpret the suffering and dying of the Lord. Now, in the celebration of the eucharist, there is a threefold cry uttered with increasing emphasis, taking up the words of John the Baptist who sees Jesus coming to him and says, 'Behold the lamb of God who takes away the sins of the world' (John 1.29).

When in the home of the cantor of the Thomaskirche in Leipzig, Mozart said that he thought that Protestants could not begin to understand what Catholics felt when they said the '*Agnus Dei*'.[86] No saints, not even Mary, are invoked as mediators in the prayers and intercessions of this hymn in the mass, but only the one Holy One himself, God's Messiah, the Lamb of God: 'Lord, have mercy'. Twice there follows the *Miserere*, which in contrast to the customary musical tradition Mozart does not set in alternation between soloists and choir but rather as a soprano solo, a bel canto. Only at the end is it taken over by contralto, tenor and bass almost as a matter of course, to lead into the tutti of the finale. Here, too, Mozart shows not only his sovereign freedom but also his theological sensitivity as a musician. The petition for mercy is presented first of all by an individual – in the form of a muted andante sostenuto. First of all the individual stands before God and asks for mercy before the choir joins in.

The change of rhythm and tempo at the conclusion is also striking. The great petition of the peoples, '*Dona nobis pacem*', now resounds in an increasingly accelerated *andante con moto*. Tradition has it that as early as 1281 a Salzburg synod added this special prayer for peace, prefacing it with the words 'Lord, give us peace.' However, in Mozart this petition becomes a confident, comforting and encouraging expression of praise motivated by thanksgiving: 'Give us peace, yes, Lord, you give us peace, redemption, bliss.'

After all this there can be no question that Mozart's church music is liturgy resounding in music without any theological reflection. And if Mozart, that master of invention and precision, can also express something theologically special, indeed truly ecumenical, in his music, it is this great Yes which is certain of salvation and confidently embraces all the negativities of life. The Protestant theologian Karl Barth, who was particularly fond of Mozart's masses and even wanted a performance of the Coronation Mass at the Assembly of the World Council of Churches in Evanston, put it like this: 'Herein is the strangely exciting but at the same time calming quality of his music: it evidently comes from on high, where (since everything is known there) the right and left of existence and therefore its joy and sorrow, good and evil, life and death, are experienced in their reality but also in their limitation.'[87]

Life and death: on 4 April 1787, only four years before his own early death, the thirty-one-year-old Wolfgang Amadeus Mozart had written to his mortally-ill father something which he had also told to friends: ' . . . I never lie down at night without reflecting that – young as I am – I may not live to see another day. Yet no one of all my acquaintances could say that in company I am morose and disgruntled. For this blessing I daily thank my Creator and wish with all my heart that each one of my fellow-creatures could enjoy it.'[88]

Notes

1 Reported by Wolfgang's father Leopold Mozart in his letter of 16 February 1785, quoted from *Letters of Mozart and his Family*, edited and translated by Emily Anderson, third revised edition by Stanley Sadie and Fiona Smart, Macmillan 1989, henceforth quoted as *Letters*. Haydn is said to have remarked: 'Before God and as an honest man I tell you that your son is the greatest composer known to me either in person or by name. He has taste, and what is more, the most profound knowledge of composition' (886). The standard German edition has been produced by the International Mozart Foundation in Salzburg, edited by J. H. Eibl on the basis of work by W. A. Bauer and O. E. Deutsch, Kassel 1962–75 (7 vols.). In addition to the letters, important information about Mozart's life is contained in O. E. Deutsch, *Mozart: A Documentary Biography*, Macmillan ²1966, and C. Eisen, *New Mozart Documents. A Supplement to O. E. Deutsch's Documentary Biography*, Macmillan 1991. Cf. Also H. C. Robbins Landon (ed.), *The Mozart Compendium. A Guide to Mozart's Life and Music*, Thames and Hudson 1990.
2 Cf. K. Barth, *Wolfgang Amadeus Mozart*, Eerdmans 1986.
3 Cf. W. Hildesheimer, *Mozart*, Dent 1983.
4 Karl Barth, *Church Dogmatics*, III.3, T. & T. Clark 1961, 298.
5 Cf. Barth, *Mozart* (n. 2), 26.
6 Cf. Hildesheimer, *Mozart* (n. 3), 361.
7 Ibid.
8 The following are important biographies by contemporaries: G. N. von Nissen, *Biographie W. A. Mozart's. Nach Originalbriefen, Sammlungen alles über ihn geschriebenen, mit*

vielen Beylagen, Steindrücken, Musikblättern und einem Facsimile, Herausgegeben von Constanze von Nissen früher Witwe Mozart, Leipzig 1828; F. Niemetschek, *Leben des k. k. Kapellmeisters Wolfgang Gottlieb Mozart nach Original-Quellen beschrieben,* Prague 1798. The foundations for historical Mozart scholarship were laid by O. Jahn's monumental two-volume biography of Mozart, *Life of Mozart,* Novello, Ewer and Co 1882 (3 vols.), which in Germany has been revised and substantially extended by the still standard biography by H. Abert, *W. A. Mozart. Neubearbeitete und erweiterte Ausgabe von Otto Jahns Mozart* (2 vols.), Leipzig 1955–6. The biography by A. Schurig, *Wolfgang Amadeus Mozart. Sein Leben und sein Werk auf Grund der vornehmlich durch Nikolaus von Nissen gesammelten biographischen Quellen und der Ergebnisse der neuesten Forschung dargestellt* (2 vols.), Leipzig 1913, is also still important. Mozart's work is divided into thirty-four periods in the stylistic investigation by T. de Wyzewa and G. de Saint-Foix, *W. A. Mozart, Sa vie musicale et son oeuvre, de l'enfance à la pleine maturité* (5 vols.), Paris 1936–46. The following more recent biographies of Mozart are important: B. Paumgartner, *Mozart,* Zurich [6]1967; A. Einstein, *Mozart. His Character and his Work* (1946), Panther Books 1971; E. Schenk, *Mozart and His Times,* Secker and Warburg 1966; J. H. Eibl, *Wolfgang Amadeus Mozart, Chronik eines Lebens,* Kassel 1965; K. Pahlen (ed.), *Das Mozart-Buch. Chronik von Leben und Werk,* Wiesbaden 1969; A. Hutchings, *Mozart: The Man – The Musician,* Schirmer 1976.

9 W. A. Mozart, letter to his father from Vienna, 9 May 1781, *Letters,* 729.

10 It is comforting to think that Mozart might have met with more understanding among present-day Salzburg Catholics, since according to opinion polls in 1990 65% of Salzburg Catholics (and even 85% of independent and leading figures) were not very, or not at all, satisfied with the ministry of the archbishop who had been forced upon them.

11 For Mozart's freemasonry cf. H.–J. Irmen, *Mozart Mitglied geheimer Gesellschaften,* Neustadt/Aisch 1976. As late as 1780 Leopold Mozart had enrolled himself and his son in the Holy Cross

Brotherhood in Salzburg in his own hand. Cf. W. Hummel, 'Das Bruderschaftsbüchl der Hl. Kreuzbruderschaft an der Bürgerspitalskirche in Salzburg', *Jahresschrift 1959 Salzburger Museum Carolino Augusteum*, Salzburg 1960, 205–21. For the reference to W. Hummel, as also for a later reference to J. Mancal, I am grateful to the Director of the Archiepiscopal Consistory Archive, Dr Ernst Hintermaier. Cf. also Paul Nettl, *Mozart and Masonry*, Philosophical Library 1956, reissued Da Capo Press, New York 1970.

12 Cf. Hildesheimer, *Mozart* (n. 3), 364.

13 Ibid., 273.

14 Ibid., 274.

15 W. A. Mozart, letter to his father from Mannheim, 4 February 1778, *Letters*, 461.

16 Thus his mother, Anna Maria Mozart, reports some days later: 'I prayed every day that God might prevent this journey and, thank Heaven, He has done so. Most people here have no religion and are out-and-out free-thinkers. No one knows that this is the reason why Wolfgang has not gone off with them, for, if it were known, we should be laughed at' (letter to Mozart's father from Mannheim, 22 February 1781, *Letters*, 489).

17 Thus Hildesheimer, *Mozart* (n. 3), 362.

18 This report, which is credible in every respect, comes from Friedrich Rochlitz, a pupil of the Thomasschule, a musicologist and founder of the *Allgemeine Musikalische Zeitung* in Leipzig. In that journal, between 1798 and 1801, he published 'authenticated anecdotes from Wolfgang Gottlieb Mozart's life'. The following quotations appear in Vol. 3, 1800/1801, 494f.

19 Cf. Barth, *Mozart* (n. 2), 17.

20 W. A. Mozart, letter to his father from Paris, 9 July 1778, *Letters*, 563.

21 Barth, *Mozart* (n. 2), 20.

22 Ibid., 16.

23 Ibid.

24 Ibid., 23.

25 Hildesheimer, *Mozart* (n. 3), 15.

26 Einstein, *Mozart* (n. 8), 14.

27 The quotation is from E. H. Flammer, *Politisch engagierte Musik als kompositorisches Problem, dargestellt am Beispiel von Luigi Nono und Hans Werner Henze*, Baden-Baden 1981, 116.

28 H. Urs von Balthasar, 'Das Abschieds-Terzett', in *Mozart. Aspekte*, ed. P. Schaller and H. Kühner, Olten 1956, 279–88: 288. The Catholic theologian even thinks that he can add: 'What everywhere else would necessarily seem to be a vain delusion or even a blasphemy, the final revelation of eternal beauty in an authentic earthly body, transcending any farewell, might here, in the Catholic incarnational sphere, even become gladdening reality' (ibid.). Von Balthasar later spoke of Mozart in a more sober way, in id., *Theodramatik* II.1, Einsiedeln 1976, 244f.

29 Before Barth, another great admirer of Mozart, the Dane Søren Kierkegaard, had used *Don Giovanni* to clarify the necessary distinction between the aesthetic, ethical and religious forms of existence; in opposition to German idealism and the German idealization of man he again firmly insisted on 'the infinite difference between God and man'.

30 Barth, *Mozart* (n.2), 43.

31 Cf. e.g. Schurig, *Wolfgang Amadeus Mozart* (n.8). G. W. Tschitscherin, the Russian musicologist (and first Foreign Minister of the young Soviet Republic under Lenin), vigorously criticized Schurig's picture of Mozart as early as 1930: id., *Mozart. Eine Studie*, new edition Reinbek bei Hamburg 1987, 60–4.

32 Hildesheimer, *Mozart* (n. 3), 6.

33 None of this is of interest to us here. Nowadays one can read enough about this human, all-too-human side of the life of the composer who is so popular today and which is popularized by every means and on all the media. One can read not only about Mozart's ambivalent relations with his strict but highly musical father, his warm-hearted but musically quite insignificant mother, and his sister Nannerl (Maria Anna), but also about his relationship with the 'little cousin' (Maria Anna Thekla) mentioned above, which was hardly just platonic, and the fifteen-year-old singer Aloysia Weber, whom he loved but who finally refused him. In her place Mozart finally married the second of the sisters,

Constanze – by and large not a bad marriage. Present-day biographers now think that this was an arrangement on the basis of 'erotic understanding' (Hildesheimer, *Mozart* [n. 3], 254).

34 American radical critics, most recently Susan McClary, even think that in the perfectly balanced G major piano concerto KV 453 (1784) they can detect a striking social alienation. This is said to be expressed in the antagonism between orchestra and soloist, whose personal needs are sacrificed to the overpowering social conventions of the orchestra; the untroubled finale is said merely to disguise the repression. If Karl Marx ever heard Mozart's music, would he have heard it in such Marxist tones? Cf. R. Taruskin, 'Consumer Mozart: From God-Child to Musical Yuppie', *International Herald Tribune*, 14 September 1990.

35 Hildesheimer, *Mozart* (n. 3), 7.

36 Cf. Hildesheimer, *Mozart* (n. 3), 315–32.

37 Cf. A. Werner-Jensen, *Reclams Musikführer. W. A. Mozart*, I. *Instrumentalmusik*, Stuttgart 1989, 208.

38 F. Busoni, *Wesen und Einheit der Musik*, a new edition of Busoni's writings and notes, revised and supplemented by J. Herrmann, Berlin 1956, 143.

39 Cf. Hildesheimer, *Mozart* (n. 3), 35–8, 44, 360.

40 Barth, *Mozart* (n. 2), 33f.

41 Ibid., 55.

42 Ibid., 22.

43 Cf. Barth, *Church Dogmatics* III.3 (n. 4), 298.

44 Cf. H. Hesse, *Steppenwolf*, Secker and Warburg 1929, reissued Penguin 1946, 238.

45 Ibid.

46 But cf. Mozart's devastating letter of 3 July 1778 from Paris to Abbé Bullinger, a friend of the family, asking him to break the news of his mother's death as gently as possible to his father, *Letters*, 559f.

47 Hildesheimer, *Mozart* (n. 3), 74, 193.

48 Thus now, in the steps of Hildesheimer, Rose Rosenguard Subotnik. Cf. Taruskin, 'Consumer Mozart' (n. 34).

49 W. A. Mozart, letter to his father of 3 July 1778 (the day of his mother's death), from Paris, in *Letters*, 558.

50 L. Mozart, letter to his son of 20 October 1777 from Salzburg, in *Letters*, 334.

51 This is noted by Hildesheimer, *Mozart* (n. 3), 314.

52 Cf. J. Mancal, 'Leopold Mozart (1719–1787). Zum 200. Todestag eines Augsburgers', in *Leopold Mozart zum 200. Todestag. Ausstellung des Stadtarchivs Augsburg. Katalog*, Augsburg 1987, 1–23.

53 Cf. I. Parhamer, *Historischer Katechismus, oder gründlicher Glaubens- und Sittenlehren aus den Geschichten der Göttlichen Schrift*, Vienna 1749.

54 P. Canisius, *Christ-katholischer Stadt- und Landkatechismus*, Graz 1722, 2. The answer to the question how the individual believes in this one, supreme, divine Majesty who is worthy of love, how he hopes for him and loves him, is: 'When he often says from the heart: O my God! You are the supreme good. You are a sole, omnipotent, eternal God. A creator of all things: a just God, who judges, rewards or punishes all according to their works. O my God! I believe in you, I hope in you, I love you, I want to serve you as long as I live and I want to be with you to eternity' (4). I am indebted for this information to Frau Dr Regina Brandl of the Institute of Catechetics and Religious Education in the Theological Faculty at the University of Innsbruck.

55 W. A. Mozart, letter to his father from Paris, 9 July 1778, *Letters*, 561. Similarly, his father Leopold recalled in his old age the difficult time after the death of his first three children: 'I took everything as it came, and always thought that God in his divine providence supplies us all things needful if we punctiliously repay our debt with love for God, our fellow men, and ourselves' (Schenck, *Mozart and his Times* [n. 8], 38).

56 W. A. Mozart, letter to his father from Vienna, 4 April 1787, *Letters*, 907.

57 Cf. Rochlitz, 'Verbürgte Anekdoten' (n. 18), 494f.

58 Hildesheimer, *Mozart* (n. 3), 340.

59 V. Braunbehrens, *Mozart in Vienna, 1781–1791*, Oxford University Press 1991, 363.

60 G. Gruber, *Mozart and Posterity*, Quartet Books 1991, 5.

61 Hildesheimer, *Mozart* (n. 3), 333.

62 W. A. Mozart, letter to his father from Vienna, 4 April 1787, *Letters*, 907.

63 For these musical examples and other suggestions I am grateful to the musicologist and composer Professor Karl Michael Komma.

64 Cf. the report by Rochlitz, 'Verbürgte Anekdoten' (n. 18), 493.

65 For a more detailed account of Mozart's death and burial cf. the remarks by V. Braunbehrens, *Mozart in Vienna* (n. 59), 403–28, which put right a number of legends.

66 Cf. Acts 17.27f.

67 Cf. H. Küng, *Does God Exist? An Answer for Today*, Collins and Doubleday 1978, reissued SCM Press and Crossroad Publishing Company 1991, F II 2 Controversy on natural theology. According to Barth's *Church Dogmatics*, III.3, 298, Mozart's music belongs just in the doctrine of creation and then again only in eschatology. K. Hammer's dissertation, *W. A. Mozart – eine theologische Deutung. Ein Beitrag zur theologischen Anthropologie*, Zurich 1964, prepared under Karl Barth and Werner Bieder, compares the ethical-anthropological expression of Mozart's music with comparable statements of biblical anthropology.

68 T. W. Adorno and E. Kogon, 'Offenbarung oder autonome Vernunft', *Frankfurter Hefte* 13, 1958, 484–98: 498.

69 Gruber, *Mozart and Posterity*, 237.

70 G. B. Shaw, quoted in Tarushkin, 'Consumer Mozart' (n. 34).

71 For Mozart's church music see K. G. Fellerer, *Mozarts Kirchenmusik*, Salzburg 1955; G. Geiringer, 'The Church Music', in *The Mozart Companion*, ed. H. C. Robbins Landon and D. Mitchell, Rockliff 1956, 361–76; P. Nettl, *W. A. Mozart*, Frankfurt 1955, 67–79: R. Teuschert on Mozart and the church; W. Senn, *Wolfgang Amadeus Mozart*, Serie I, Geistliche Gesangwerke, Kassel, 1975.

72 For Mozart's time in Salzburg see E. Hintermaier, *Die Salzburger Hofkapelle von 1700 bis 1806. Organisation und Personal*, Salzburg dissertation 1972; F. Hölböck, *Wolfgang Amadeus Mozart. Der Salzburger Domorganist und seine Beziehungen zur katholischen Kirche*, Stein am Rhein 1978; M. H. Schmid, *Mozart und die Salzburger Tradition*, Tutzing 1976; C. F. von Sterneck,

Studien über W. A. Mozart. Der Freundeskreis in Salzburg, ed. J. E. Engel, Salzburg 1896.

73 Cf. F. Martin, 'Hieronymus Graf von Colloredo (1772–1803)', in id., *Salzburgs Fürsten in der Barockzeit (1578–1812)*, Salzburg ²1952, 225–56.

74 W. A. Mozart, letter to P. G. Martini, 4 September 1776, *Letters*, 266.

75 W. A. Mozart, letter to his father, 23 September 1777, *Letters*, 272.

76 For a historical explanation of the different elements in the ordinary of the Roman mass, cf. J. A. Jungmann, *Missarium Sollemnia. Eine genetische Erklärung der römischer Messe*, Vienna ²1949.

77 K. Hammer, *W. A. Mozart – eine theologische Deutung. Ein Beitrag zur theologischen Anthropologie*, Zurich 1964, 355.

78 F. X. Witt, quoted in Fellerer, *Mozarts Kirchenmusik* (n. 71), 11.

79 H. Hucke, 'Kirchenmusik', in *Das grosse Lexikon der Musik*, ed. M. Honegger and G. Massenkeil, IV, Freiburg 1964, 355.

80 Hammer, *W. A. Mozart* (n. 77), 124.

81 W. A. Mozart, letter to his father from Vienna, 9 May 1781, *Letters*, 729.

82 H. Küng, *Does God Exist?*, C. I God – a projection of man? Ludwig Feuerbach.

83 Cf. ibid., C. II God – a consolation serving vested interests? Karl Marx.

84 Cf. Fellerer, *Mozarts Kirchenmusik* (n. 71), 10.

85 Cf. H. Küng, *Does God Exist?*, D. I The rise of nihilism: Friedrich Nietzsche.

86 For an interpretation of this dictum cf. above, 'Theme 2: Religious?'

87 Barth, *Mozart* (n. 2), 33.

88 W. A. Mozart, letter to his father from Vienna, 4 April 1787, *Letters*, 907.

Index